Short ish Walks on Exmoor

Robert Hesketh

Bossiney Books

All the walks in this book were checked prior to publication, at which time the instructions were correct. However, changes can occur in the countryside over which neither the author nor the publisher has any control. Please let us know if you encounter any serious problems.

This new edition 2012
Bossiney Books Ltd, 33 Queens Drive, Ilkley, LS29 9QW
www.bossineybooks.com
First published 2005
Copyright © 2005 and 2012 Robert Hesketh   All rights reserved
ISBN 978-1-906474-36-2

Acknowledgements
The maps are by Nick Hawken
Cover design by Heards Design Partnership
The boots on the front cover were kindly supplied by The Brasher Boot Company
All photographs are by the author or from the publishers' own collection
Printed in Great Britain by R Booth Ltd, Penryn, Cornwall

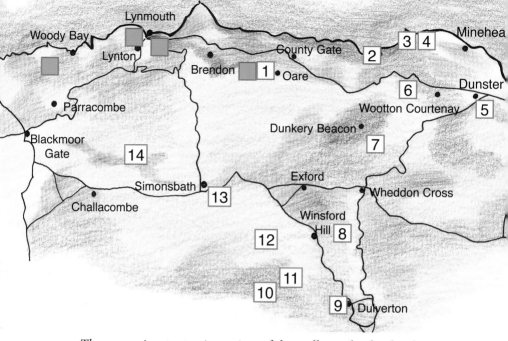

The approximate starting points of the walks in this book. The green squares represent walks in the companion title, Shortish walks in north Devon.

Introduction

This is an invitation to England's smallest National Park, a walker's paradise. High moorland and sea cliffs, rolling hills cut by fast-flowing rivers and steep wooded valleys – Exmoor is endlessly enjoyable. It is also the last stronghold of England's largest mammal, the red deer, and home to its own breed of wild ponies.

The walks in this book are typically 6-9 km (4-6 miles) in length and can be walked in a morning or an afternoon. Two are shorter, one slightly longer. The time you need will depend on how fast you walk and how interested you are in what you see on the way.

Safety (please take seriously)

Walking Exmoor is safe and trouble free – provided you are prepared. In the first place, Exmoor weather can change suddenly. As well as enjoying a generally mild climate, we also know about high winds and fogs, and it has been known to rain here too. Don't walk beside a river if it's in flood!

Wild Red deer near the Punchbowl, Winsford

Please do not set out without good walking boots and suitable clothing. Drinking water, map and compass, plus waterproofs and an extra layer, are equally essential, as well as a comfortable rucksack. Many, including me, add a walking stick, food and a mobile phone (though reception is patchy).

Ticks are a potential nuisance, especially in hot, humid weather. Wearing long trousers tucked into socks offers some protection against these tiny parasites, which can carry a viral infection, Lyme disease. If one attaches itself to you, remove it promptly and carefully with tweezers, being careful not to leave any of it in your skin, in order to minimise the risk of infection.

Maps

The sketch maps in this book are just that – sketches. For safety and interest, you should take with you the Ordnance Survey Explorer OL9 map, especially on the high moor.

Access

Unenclosed areas of Exmoor are generally open. Please keep to the paths over enclosed farmland, leave gates open or closed as you find them, and keep dogs under control, especially in the bird nesting and lambing season.

Robert Hesketh

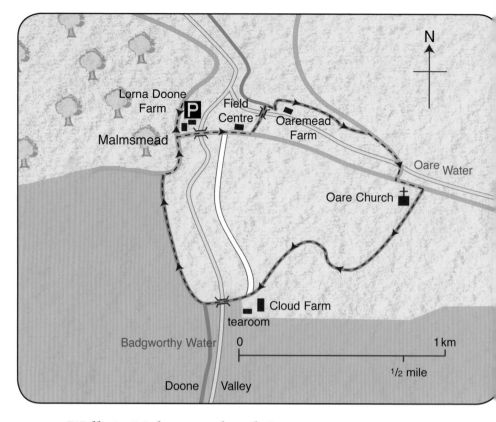

Walk 1   Malmsmead and Oare

Length: 4.2 km (2 1/2 miles) Duration of walk: 1 1/4 hours.
Can be extended.
Character: A short riverside and moorland edge route, by bridleways,
footpaths and quiet lanes. Oare church, Doone Valley and Malmsmead
feature in R D Blackmore's classic novel, Lorna Doone *(1869).*

Turn left out of the car park at Lorna Doone Farm, with its gift shop
and refreshments, the probable site of 'Plover's Barrow Farm', Jan
Ridd's home in the novel. Cross the bridge and walk past the Exmoor
Natural History Society Field Centre (limited summer opening). Take
the bridleway left for COUNTY GATE OARE.

   Cross the footbridge, turn right then immediately left, following the
path behind Oaremead Farm (OARE CHURCH). Keep to the blue waymarks and continue up the riverside track.

   On reaching the lane, turn right for Oare church, where Carver
Doone shot Lorna on her wedding day. Blackmore's memorial is in
the church, noted too for its Norman font and box pews.

4

Doone valley where, in the novel, the outlaw Doone clan had their stronghold, led by the disgruntled Scottish nobleman Sir Ensor Doone, a fugitive from the world that had rejected him. They terrorised the neighbourhood, until Jan Ridd and justice triumphed.

Turn right out of the church. At the far end of the churchyard, take the BRIDLEWAY SOUTH COMMON LARKBARROW. Walk uphill through two fields, keeping the hedge on your right.

Continue in the same line (CLOUD FARM DOONE VALLEY) keeping the fence and trees on your right, then at the next fingerpost turn right for DOONE VALLEY. Follow the path ahead to a gate. Turn right, then after 50m left (FOOTPATH). The path then drops into Doone Valley. Enter Cloud Farm's yard, and pass through the car park outside the tea rooms.

Walk ahead into Doone Valley.

Muster your courage and cross the footbridge. (If you want to extend the walk turn left and follow the path up the valley as far as you want.) Turn right onto BRIDLEWAY MALMSMEAD. Follow this through the gate with the blue spot and along a track parallel to the river. On reaching the lane, turn right back to Malmsmead.

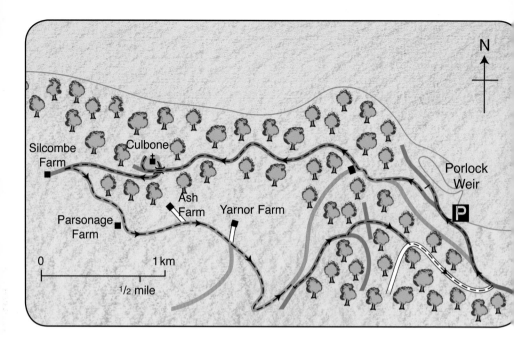

Walk 2 Porlock Weir and Culbone

Length: 9 km (5 1/2 miles)   Duration of walk: 3 hours
Character: A fairly energetic walk along woodland paths and quiet
lanes. Culbone's charming church is said to be the smallest and least
accessible in England.

Turn right out of Porlock Weir car park. Walk past the harbour and
workshops to a footpath junction. Turn left up steps onto COASTPATH
CULBONE. At the top of the steps turn right.

On reaching the lane turn right. Just under 200 m ahead, turn right
at the thatched tollhouse for CULBONE. The path passes under two
bridges and into deep woodland, once the site of oak felling and char-
coal burning. The original burners were said to be lepers, who lived
and worked in the woods until they died.

Ahead, the path has been re-routed up steps because of a landslide.
Follow the new path up steps. Keep left onto a track for 30 m, then
carry on up the zig-zags from the CULBONE CHURCH sign. The path
levels off, drops a little, then rises again to a second footpath diversion. Follow the signs for CULBONE CHURCH.

The church is on the right of the main path. Still lit by candles and
a Tilley lamp, it has an ancient door with a sanctuary ring, a Norman
font, modern iron candelabra and a box pew for the squire's family.

Leave by the gate at the upper left end of the churchyard, signed

6

COUNTY GATE/SILCOMBE. The path climbs steeply under a bridge and through a bluebell wood. At the next path junction, turn left for COAST PATH SILCOMBE FARM LYNMOUTH.

On reaching the lane, turn left for PORLOCK WEIR BY ROAD. Fine views of Wales open out as you follow the lane past Parsonage Farm, its laterally vented chimneystacks so characteristic of the region.

Now follow a series of signs to PORLOCK WEIR. At a road junction, walk straight ahead, then round a hairpin bend. Take the next public footpath on the right and keep ahead at the bridleway junction (NB do not turn left here down Worthy Combe). Follow this broad track as it curves right to the next fingerpost: turn left BRIDLEWAY PORLOCK WEIR. Cross over at the next path junction and continue ahead, as indicated by blue paint marks on the trees, to a roughly tarred lane. Bear left, and continue downhill to a road. Turn left along the road back to the car park.

This window, possibly Saxon, can be seen from the back of the church.

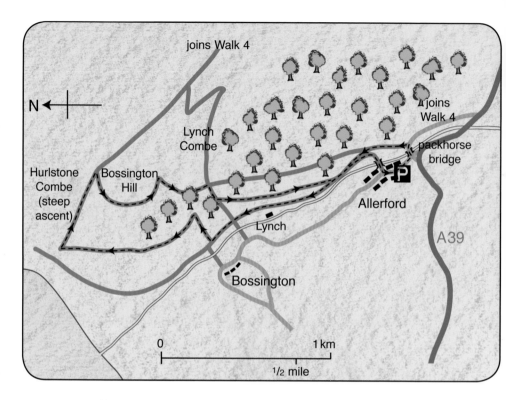

Walk 3   Allerford, Bossington and Hurlstone Combe

Length: 6 km (3³/₄ miles)   Duration of walk: 2¹/₄ hours
Character: Well signed paths through fields, moorland and woods. Two
steep ascents. Lots of benches from which to enjoy the superb views of
Dunkery, Porlock Bay and South Wales.

Turn right out of Allerford car park. Turn left over the 17th century
packhorse bridge, a reminder of transport on Exmoor when wheeled
vehicles were unknown and trains of laden horses carried goods.

Just 50m up the lane, turn left, FOOTPATH BOSSINGTON. Cross a
field to enter a wood through a gate. After 25 m when the path divides,
bear left. This path joins a track running parallel to a stream, then
climbs. Bear left BOSSINGTON.

At the next complex junction take the yellow waymarked FOOTPATH
BOSSINGTON straight ahead. If you want to visit this pretty village,
make a diversion left and down hill at the next BOSSINGTON sign.
Otherwise, walk ahead across the field to a gate. Turn right and walk
steeply uphill to a path junction: turn sharp left, HURLSTONE POINT.
The path levels off and wonderful views open out.

Allerford packhorse bridge, starting point for this walk and Walk 4. The two walks could be combined.

Both this walk and Walk 4 provide splendid viewpoints over Porlock Bay and across the Bristol Channel to Wales.

After nearly 1km, at the next junction, turn right COASTPATH MINEHEAD. This leads steeply up Hurlstone Combe. On reaching the top, turn right for LYNCH COMBE. Follow this beautiful high-level path along the contour line around the rim of Lynch Combe and down into the woods.

When you cross another path, turn right downhill (BOSSINGTON) for about 200m, then turn left through a gate (ALLERFORD). Continue ahead, taking the right, downhill, path at each fork, and you will reach a stream: cross a footbridge into Allerford. Walk through a farmyard, then turn left along the village street back to your car.

9

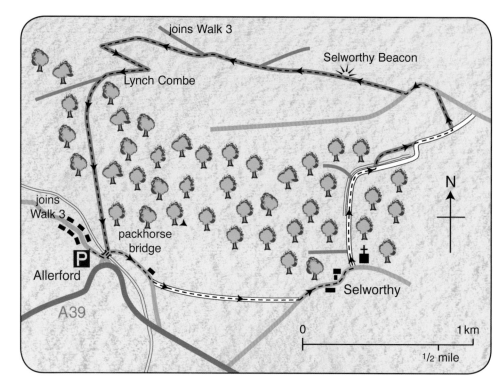

Walk 4 Allerford and Selworthy Beacon

Length: 7.5km (4¹/₂ miles)   Duration of walk: 2¹/₄ hours
Character: Field, woodland and moorland paths. Wonderful views of
high Exmoor, Porlock Bay and the coast beyond. Allerford's packhorse
bridge and museum, as well as Selworthy's church and thatched
buildings, add greatly to the interest.

Turn right out of Allerford car park. Only 50m ahead, turn left over
the 17th century packhorse bridge. Follow the lane ahead. It curves
right, but when it curves right again by a thatched cottage, walk
straight ahead up a a stony track.

On reaching Selworthy, bear left past the 14th century tithe barn
with its animal symbols. Turn left at the brown wooden gate to visit
the tearooms and the National Trust Information Centre and shop
(seasonal opening).

Walk on to Selworthy's beautiful limewashed church. It has many
interesting features, including a Norman font, fine gallery, handsome
pulpit, many monuments and wonderful roof bosses. Few churches
enjoy a more impressive setting – the views of Dunkery and the surrounding moorland are stunning.

10

Turn right out of the church and take the bridleway right signed SELWORTHY BEACON/BURY CASTLE. Ignore the turning left for BURY CASTLE and walk up the right side of the brook, SELWORTHY BEACON. Ignore the broad path left to SELWORTHY BEACON. Continue ahead, also signed SELWORTHY BEACON. The track curves to the right; take the narrow path on the left, crossing the brook. Continue ahead (BRIDLEWAY) onto the open moor.

At the next junction, turn left for SELWORTHY BEACON and bear left, then join the lane for 150 m. Bear right onto the broad track up to Selworthy Beacon. At 308 m (over 1000 ft) the beacon is a magnificent viewpoint, overlooking South Wales and a vast tract of Exmoor and the coast.

Do not divert left towards the lane but walk ahead on the broad ridge track, which is joined by the Coast Path. When the track divides, fork left away from the Coast Path, for BOSSINGTON AND LYNCH.

Continue left for Lynch at the next sign. A splendid view of Porlock Bay opens out. The path descends. Turn sharp left, BRIDLEWAY. The path curves down to a sign BRIDLEWAY LYNCH COMBE. Turn right here and walk downhill. At the next path junction turn left, through a gate, for ALLERFORD. This path leads gently down through the woods to the packhorse bridge and the car park.

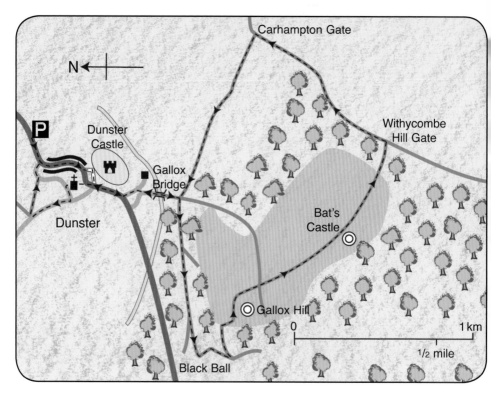

Walk 5   Dunster and Bat's Castle

Length 7.7 km: (4³/₄ miles)   Duration of walk: 2¹/₄ hours
Character: A walk packed with interest. We visit Dunster's yarn
market, castle, watermill, packhorse bridge, priory church, tithe barn,
dovecote and butter cross, as well as two Iron Age hillforts. There are
wonderful views of the town, of Exmoor and of the Bristol Channel.

From the car park at the north end of Dunster, turn left, and walk past
the Information Centre into the main street, dominated by the medieval Luttrell Arms (once the Abbot of Cleve's house), the octagonal
yarn market (1609) and the castle. This retains its 13th century gate-
house, but was remodelled in 1872 for the Luttrell family.

Walk straight on towards the castle (National Trust). Either visit the
castle now, or turn right down to West Street. Turn left down West
Street and left again for WATER MILL. Follow the mill leat down to the
sign GALLOX BRIDGE. To visit the 18th century mill (fully restored)
walk ahead. Otherwise turn right, then keep left past thatched cottages and cross medieval Gallox Bridge.

Walk ahead past a pair of thatched cottages and take the uphill
track, TIMBERSCOMBE LUXBOROUGH VIA CROYDON HILL. When the

track divides, keep ahead, BAT'S CASTLE CIRCUIT. Walk past VIEWPOINT (or divert to see the view). Stay on BAT'S CASTLE CIRCUIT until you reach a sharp left turn DEER PARK CIRCUIT. Follow this uphill to a track junction. Keep right and uphill DEER PARK CIRCUIT. Black Ball camp (Iron Age) is on your right as you emerge from the trees, but partly hidden by bracken.

Continue on the same footpath to Bat's Castle, where the rubble of the Iron Age stone ramparts is clearly visible. At 213 m above sea level, this is a fine viewpoint and defensive position. Walk on in the same direction, passing a small earthwork then descending through trees to WITHYCOMBE HILL GATE.

Do not take the Dunster path. Go through the gate and turn left, PATH TO CARHAMPTON. After about 600 m, turn left through a small gate onto FOOTPATH TO DUNSTER. Walk on, keeping the field boundary on your right and enjoying the view of the castle.

Retrace your steps over Gallox Bridge and into West Street to visit the former priory church with its 1499 carved screen and Luttrell family monuments. Leave by the north door. Beyond the Garden of Remembrance are the medieval dovecote and a barn.

With your back to the garden gate, turn left. Turn right at the school and walk uphill to the medieval butter cross. Turn right PUBLIC FOOTPATH and follow the path which leads across a field towards the sea. Reaching a lane, walk ahead, then turn left at the main road, back to the car park.

13

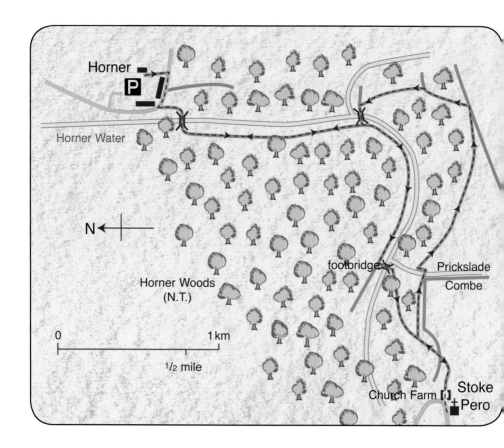

Walk 6   Horner Woods and Stoke Pero

Length: 8.6 km (5 1/2 miles) Duration of walk: 3 hours
Character: Ancient oak woodland. Full of wild flowers in spring, it
offers shade in summer, rich colours in autumn and a good chance of
seeing Red deer. Stoke Pero has a charming church. One very steep and
long ascent.

Begin at Horner's National Trust car park. The information board by
the toilets describes the many interesting features of Horner Woods,
including the archaeology and wildlife. This huge area is crisscrossed
with paths, so please attend to directions.

Take the path from the information board out to the road and turn
right past the tearooms. Notice the red tiles and laterally vented chimneystacks, characteristic of Somerset. Turn left for HORNER WOODS.
Follow the broad track ahead, then over the bridge and upstream,
keeping Horner Water on your left.

14

Continue for 2.7 km, ignoring side turnings, until you reach a path junction for GRANNY'S RIDE STOKE PERO. Turn left and cross the footbridge. Take the steep path uphill. Ignore turnings to the left. Keep right at the signs BRIDLEWAY STOKE PERO. This leads to an enclosed lane and through the yard of Church Farm to Stoke Pero church.

The name is derived from *stoc* (outlying enclosure) and Pyrow, the Norman family granted the land after the Conquest. At 309 m above sea level, Stoke Pero is the highest church on Exmoor.

Retrace your steps past the last fingerpost and back through the gate. About 200 m further on, at a tree with a blue arrow painted on it (which could be hard to see if it's gloomy), the path divides. Bear right (PERMITTED FOOTPATH CLOUTSHAM BALL) on a grassy path towards but not through a gate. Follow the path along the edge of the woods to Prickslade Combe.

Turn left down the combe, then turn right across the stream and continue just inside the edge of the woods. At the next path junction continue on BRIDLEWAY. After 80 m the path divides again. Bear left, downhill. At the next path division keep left, descending gently along a ridge and then more steeply down to East Water Valley.

At the bottom, turn left and walk to a footbridge. Cross over, keep left for a few metres, then turn right onto the broad track and retrace your steps to the car park.

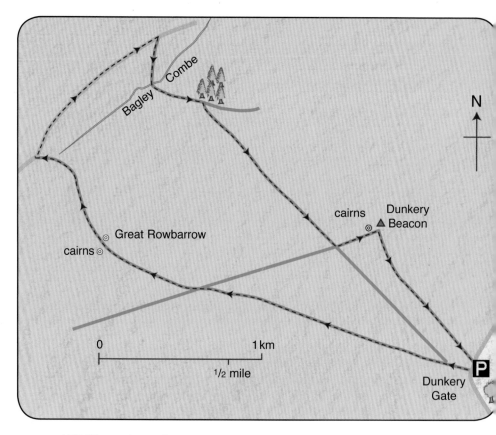

Walk 7 Dunkery Beacon

Length: 7.5 km (4 1/2 miles)   Duration of walk: 2 1/2 hours
Character: The modest effort required to walk up Dunkery Beacon –
at 512m (1704 ft) Exmoor's highest point – is richly rewarded.
Choose a clear day: the views are superb. There are several interesting
Bronze Age cairns on the way.

Park at Dunkery Gate (SS896406) below the unmistakable mass of
heather-clad Dunkery Beacon, brown in winter, green in summer
and purple in early autumn. Take the bridleway in front of you for
EXFORD. Ignore the path which forks off to the right. After 1.6km a
track joins from the right (coming down from the Beacon). Just 50m
further on, fork right onto a thinner path through the heather up to
Rowbarrow, where the Bronze Age cairns are some 3500 to 4000
years old. Continue ahead, enjoying the view over the Bristol
Channel to Wales.

One of the Bronze Age cairns on Rowbarrow, with Dunkery Beacon in the distance

On reaching a lane, turn right and walk on for 1.1 km to a finger post on the right, DICKY'S PATH WEBBER'S POST. Follow the track down into Bagley Combe and up the other side. Fork right opposite a small stand of fir trees onto a stony and unsigned track leading up to Dunkery Beacon. This merges with a bridleway and continues uphill.

At a 'crossroads' on the shoulder of Dunkery Beacon turn left and walk up to the conical summit cairn. This was built in 1935 to commemorate the gift of Dunkery to the National Trust by Sir Thomas Acland. Do not confuse it with the Bronze Age cairns nearby.

The panorama is immense, ranging from the coast and mountains of South Wales along the Bristol Channel to the Quantocks. Exmoor lies before you like a map and Dartmoor can be seen on a clear day. Use the viewing table to check what you see.

Take the broad track which initially leads South, back to Dunkery Gate.

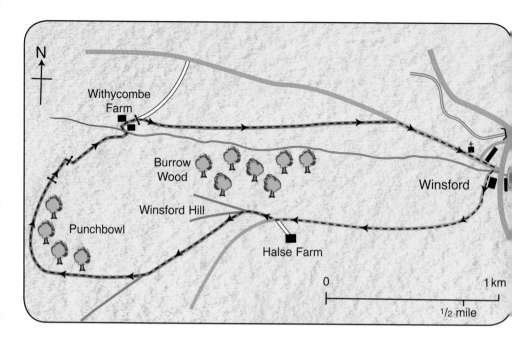

Walk 8 Winsford and the Punchbowl

Length: 6.4km (4 miles) Duration of walk: 2 hours
Character: Lanes, footpaths and open moor – compass recommended.
A steep ascent and a steep descent are rewarded by magnificent views.
Look out for Exmoor ponies and Red deer.

Winsford is an exceptionally pretty village with seven bridges. Park by
the war memorial. Facing the memorial, turn left and walk past the
thatched Royal Oak. Follow Halse Lane uphill for 1.6km. Bear right,
just after the signed turning on the opposite side to Halse Farm, onto
the open moor of Winsford Hill, which is criss-crossed with tracks.

Take the left-hand (and steepest) of the tracks ahead of you, following a WSW course. After 650m the track divides. Fork right and walk
West, following the track around the rim of the Punchbowl – a steep
and dramatic chasm some 170m (560ft) deep. The view into the
Punchbowl and on to Dunkery Beacon is stunning.

Follow the track round the northern rim of the Punchbowl to a
wooden gate. Keep the hedge on your right and follow the blue waymarks to the Withycombe sign at the next gate in the hedge on the
right, then keep the hedge on your left as you descend to Withycombe
Farm – but watch for deer. I had one of my best ever sightings here, a
group of a dozen hinds and their stag. You may also start pheasants,
which are reared in large numbers.

18

Looking into the Punchbowl

Exmoor ponies grazing on Winsford Hill

Stick to the blue waymarks through Withycombe Farm and take the track uphill. Just ten metres beyond the farm gate, turn right on PUBLIC FOOTPATH WINSFORD which follows a hedge on the right and continues through fields, gates and stiles by a series of yellow way-marks for 1.3 km to a lane. Turn right for Winsford, making a short diversion on the signed footpath to the church. Like many Somerset and Devon churches, Winsford's owes its fine late medieval stonework to prosperity brought by the wool trade. It has a handsome Norman font, a Jacobean pulpit, altar rail and coat of arms.

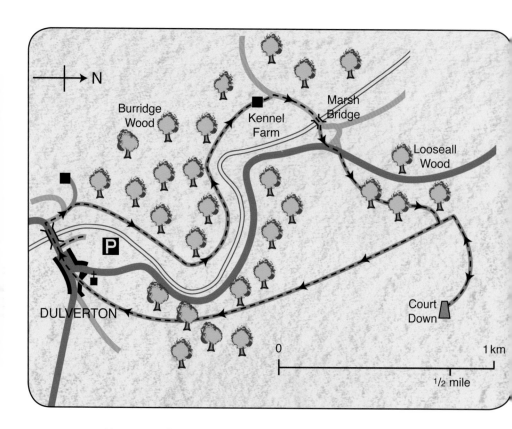

Walk 9   Dulverton and Court Down

Length: 5.7 km (3¹/₂ miles) Duration of walk: 2¹/₄ hours
Character: Riverside, woodland and open down. Superb views from
Court Down compensate for the stiff climb.

Turn left out of the car park by the National Park offices in Dulverton. Cross Dulverton's handsome bridge. It is an ancient structure, repaired 'in the yeare of our Lord God 1684' and widened by five feet in 1819 to accommodate the increase in wheeled traffic on Exmoor.

   Turn almost immediately right onto the lane signed BEECH TREE CROSS. After 125 m turn right into a signed public footpath.

   50 m further on fork right for TARR STEPS AND HAWKRIDGE. Follow this broad path through the trees and close to the river, ignoring diversions to the left, for 2 km.

   When the path divides, keep right, MARSH BRIDGE. Turn right into the lane at Kennel Farm (FOOTPATH TARR STEPS CONTINUES) which brings you to the river.

Cross Marsh Bridge and the tiny footbridge to the right of it on the far bank. Walk straight on for 50 m. Cross the road and take the footpath more or less ahead of you (RESTRICTED BYWAY COURT DOWN NORTHCOTE). Follow the path uphill for 1 km to a junction. Turn left, WINSFORD. Go through a metal gate and turn immediately right for Court Down. Walk uphill, keeping the beech hedgebank (so characteristic of Exmoor) on your right.

Go through the wooden gate on the right, 300 m ahead. Cut diagonally across the field (FOOTPATH CHILLY BRIDGE) to the old Ordnance Survey triangulation pillar on Court Down. Making maps by triangulation is history in our age of satellites and computers, but happily the 'trig pillars' remain. They offer magnificent views. At 316 m (1036 ft) above sea level, Court Down is no exception. It offers a huge Exmoor panorama, including Anstey Common, Winsford Hill and Dunkery Beacon. Dartmoor's rugged edge can be seen on a clear day.

Retrace your steps to the path junction and follow the track for DULVERTON. On reaching the church, noted for its 13th century tower and clock of 1708, turn right down the steps to the attractive Square. The Visitor Centre on the right is worth a diversion, then carry on down towards the bridge and the car park.

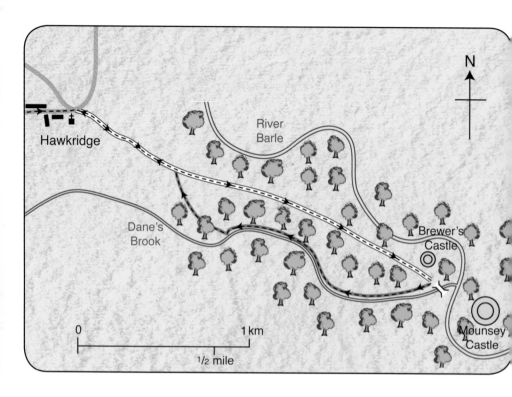

Walk 10 Hawkridge and Brewer's Castle

Length: 5.4 km (3 ¼ miles)   Duration of walk: 2 hours
Character: Quiet woodland and riverside walk, all off-road, with fine
views of East Anstey Common and the Barle Valley. A likely area to
see deer. Historic church and Iron Age fort, both worth exploring.

Park by the village hall in Hawkridge (SS 860307). At nearly 305 m
(1000 ft) above sea level, this remains one of the most isolated and
unspoilt corners of Exmoor.

Take the Tarr Steps road to visit St Giles Church. Mainly fourteenth
and fifteenth century, it has a Norman font and south doorway. Note
too the stone coffin lid, inscribed in Norman French rather than the
then prevailing Latin.

Enjoy the views over East Anstey Common and into Devon from
the churchyard. Turn right from the churchyard gate. At the far end of
the churchyard, continue ahead on RESTRICTED BYWAY DULVERTON.

800 m and two gates ahead, there is a footpath junction. Continue
for CASTLE BRIDGE, DULVERTON. After another 800 m the path begins
to descend quite steeply and (through a gate) enters woodland.

22

St Giles Church, Hawkridge, the focal point of a remote community and a great viewpoint

Just beyond the turning for the riverside path (closed at the time of writing) an unmarked path leads up through the trees to Brewer's Castle.

Together with Mounsey Castle on the opposite bank of the Barle, Brewer's Castle has a Norman name. However, the castles were built during the Iron Age to guard the ford below, at what is now Castle Bridge on the ancient trackway between Dulverton and Hawkridge, part of which you have just walked.

Both castles are overgrown and eroded, but their shape and ramparts can still be discerned.

Follow the main track down to Castle Bridge. Do not cross the bridge. Turn right for ANSTEY COMMON. This clearly defined bridleway follows Dane's Brook. At the next bridleway junction, turn right as signed BRIDLEWAY HAWKRIDGE.

Follow the path uphill through trees to a wall. Bear left uphill, keeping the wall on your right. Turn left at the next waymark, HAWKRIDGE. Retrace your steps to the church.

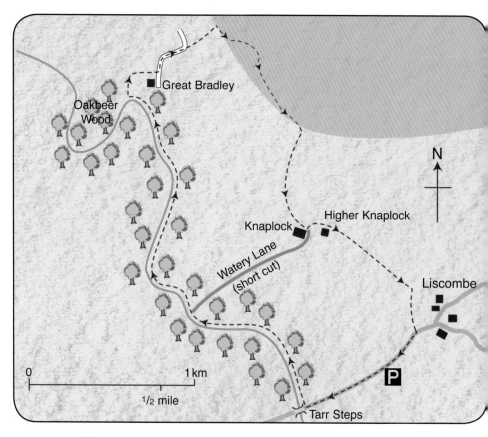

Knaplock   Higher Knaplock

Watery Lane (short cut)

Oakbeer Wood

Great Bradley

Liscombe

Tarr Steps

0   1 km   1/2 mile

N

Walk 11   Tarr Steps, Oakbeer Wood and Knaplock

Length: 7.2 km (4 1/2 miles)   Duration of walk: 2 1/4 hours
Character: We take a beautiful wooded riverside path out, and
a moorland edge route back. Tarr Steps is one of Exmoor's most
fascinating historic structures. One steepish ascent. Some parts very
muddy after rain. Do not attempt the walk if the river is very high.

Turn left out of the Tarr Steps car park, taking the footpath (not the
lane) downhill to Tarr Steps. This magnificent clapper bridge is 36 m
wide, with 17 slabs of flat stone, each weighing up to two tonnes and
over 2 m long. Most authorities now agree Tarr Steps is medieval, not
older than the 13th century, but the ford may have been used by a
prehistoric trackway.

    Turn right before crossing, and follow the east bank of the Barle
upriver. If you wish to shorten the walk to about 4 km, turn right up
Watery Lane to Knaplock after 1.2 km. Otherwise, continue upriver
on the permitted path for a further 1.6 km, to a triangular path junction.

24

Turn right on BRIDLEWAY TO WINSFORD HILL and walk uphill. At the next path junction, carry on over the ford for WINSFORD HILL. Follow the clearly defined path and blue waymarks around Great Bradley to a tarmac lane. Turn left up to Higher Bradley.

Cross the cattle grid and bear right off the lane (WINSFORD HILL KNAPLOCK) following a turf track parallel to the hedge for 200 m to a fingerpost.

Continue ahead, KNAPLOCK. Follow the next sign, BRIDLEWAY AVOIDING BOG, as it diverges from the old path near the wall. Continue ahead at the next sign TARR STEPS VIA KNAPLOCK, which winds back to rejoin the old path.

Walk on using the wall and the well defined track as your guides. At Knaplock, ignore the paths downhill to TARR STEPS. Turn left instead, BRIDLEWAY WINSFORD HILL. 150 m ahead at Higher Knaplock, take the footpath ahead for TARR STEPS VIA LISCOMBE.

Keep the hedge on your right as you follow yellow waymarks through several fields. After a multiple stile, bear slightly right across the field to a metal gate. Turn right after the gate over a stile. Cut diagonally left across the first field, then left along the track. On reaching the tarmac lane, turn right and walk back to the car park. (This lane can be busy in high season, so take care.)

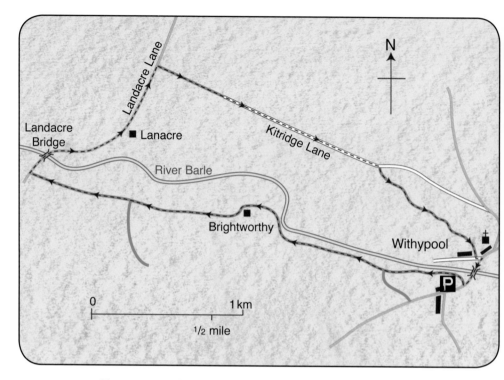

Walk 12 Withypool and Landacre Bridge

Length: 7.3 km (4 1/2 miles)   Duration of walk: 2 1/4 hours
Character: Beautiful riverside and moorland edge paths and quiet
lanes. Two handsome bridges add to the interest. One stiff ascent and
fifteen stiles compensated for by wonderful views of the Barle Valley
and surrounding moorland.

Park in the signed parking area next to Withypool's arched bridge
(SS 845354). Built in traditional style with stone in 1866, it is one of
Exmoor's newer bridges. Don't cross: turn left on the bankside path to
LANDACRE.

The well-beaten route passes through a series of fields with stiles
and yellow waymarks. When faced with a choice of yellow waymarks,
ignore the path through a narrow gate and continue along the valley,
LANDACRE BRIDGE. Duckboards help with damp sections. After
1.4 km bear left away from the river, signed LANDACRE, and climb up
to Brightworthy.

Follow the path round the back of the farm and continue uphill as
signed keeping the hedgebank on your right, up an old drove track.
On reaching the open moor, keep straight ahead. (Do not turn left

26

Landacre is Exmoor's oldest arched bridge

towards Withypool Common.) Follow the beaten path over the turf to meet the tarmac lane. Turn right and cross Landacre Bridge, which appears in RD Blackmore's *Lorna Doone* as the scene of one of Tom Faggus's daring escapes. Considered Exmoor's oldest arched bridge, Landacre was repaired as early as 1621 and again in 1828. The repairs then cost £31 – including ten shillings 'for the liquor for the Men at the Time they was Turning the Water.'

Continue up the lane, past Lanacre Farm. Turn right for WITHYPOOL when you reach the open moor. At first the track (part of the Two Moors Way from Ivybridge to Lynton) goes over turf. Metalled, it continues as Kitridge Lane.

After 2 km turn right at the stile for WITHYPOOL. Go through the narrow field then follow the beaten path downhill via yellow way-marks. On reaching the village, turn left then immediately right over the bridge to your car.

Alternatively, turning left and going straight on brings you to the Royal Oak and the attractive church with its cable moulded Norman font.

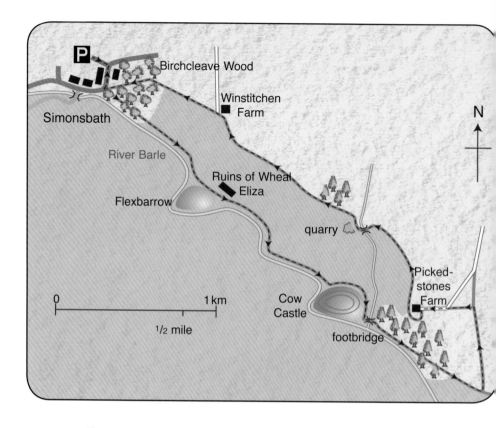

Walk 13   Simonsbath and the Barle Valley

Length: 10.8km (6³/4 miles) – the longest in this book
Duration of walk: 3¹/4 hours
Character: This section of the Barle Valley is exceptionally dramatic
and beautiful. We follow the river via Wheal Eliza mine and Cow
Castle hillfort and return by a high-level route with fine views
of the valley.

Park at the signed car park in Simonsbath. Walk back to the road and
turn right. At the foot of the slope, turn left onto the Two Moors Way
for COW CASTLE PICKEDSTONES. After 20 m bear right, COW CASTLE.
Follow the well beaten path through Birchcleave, a mature beech
wood, and behind Flexbarrow to Wheal Eliza. Like many enterprises
on Exmoor this mine was the work of entrepreneurs John and Fredric
Knight. Fredric Knight's miners drove a 75m deep shaft at Wheal
Eliza. Looking for copper, they found iron ore, but the mine was never
profitable. It closed in 1857.

Do not cross the footbridge but continue along the north bank of

the river to Cow Castle, the most impressive Iron Age hillfort on Exmoor.

(You could climb a rough path to the summit, which would add 20 minutes, a short distance and considerable effort to the walk!)

Follow the Two Moors Way over a stile and a small footbridge. Walk ahead through trees on the north bank, following signs for WITHYPOOL and PICKEDSTONES. After leaving the trees, turn left at the next path junction onto DIVERTED BRIDLEWAY. Climb steadily with the hedge on your left. At the next path junction, turn left through a gate for PICKEDSTONES. At the tarmac track turn left, BRIDLEWAY PICKED-STONES SIMONSBATH.

At Pickedstones take the PUBLIC BRIDLEWAY SIMONSBATH to the left of the buildings. Follow the well worn path with the hedge on your right and look down into the valley for a bird's eye view of Cow Castle and its ramparts. Keep left where the track forks just after a gate and descend to a brook and an old quarry, then climb again. Turn left for SIMONSBATH at the next fingerpost. Continue uphill with the trees and then a hedge on your right. At the next fingerpost, turn right for SIMONSBATH. Do not walk up the tarmac track but bear left, BRIDLEWAY SIMONSBATH. Walk on through a series of fields following the blue waymarks.

Re-entering Birchcleave Wood, turn left, SIMONSBATH and follow the path down to the road. Turn right to the car park.

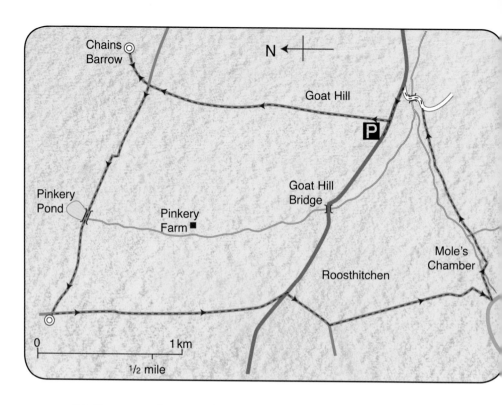

Walk 14   Pinkery and Mole's Chamber

Length: 9.7 km (6 miles)   Duration of walk: 3 hours
Character: Superb views of the moor, South Wales and Bideford Bay.
We visit Pinkery Pond – a 3 hectare (7 acre) lake – and two of
Exmoor's finest prehistoric burial chambers, and walk part of an
ancient road, the Harepath. Wet ground. Walking boots and compass
essential.

Park in the parking area beside the B3358 at SS 729401. From the eastern (Simonsbath) end take the BRIDLEWAY CHAINS BARROW. Follow the blue markers across two fields, keeping the wall on your right. Continue through a wooden gate on the same course, using the blue marker posts as a guide. (Some had fallen at the time of writing.)

At a path junction, go through a gate, bear right, and walk for 330 m to the triangulation pillar on CHAINS BARROW.

At 487 m this Bronze Age burial mound is one of the highest points on Exmoor. However, the Chains is Exmoor's rainy watershed. Its thin soil, dominated by deer sedge, is often waterlogged.

Retrace your steps to the path junction. Turn right, PINKERY POND. Keep the fence on your right up to a gate, then walk on with the fence

on your left. Pinkworthy (always pronounced and sometimes spelt Pinkery) dams the infant River Barle. Irish labourers dug it at the behest of Exmoor landowner John Knight in the early 19th century. John Knight's reasons for constructing Pinkery Pond are unknown; it may have been to power mining machinery, or just to make an impressive landscape feature.

Walk along the dam wall and on via a gate to the far right corner of the enclosure at Woodbarrow, another Bronze Age mound. Turn left for B3358 ROAD. Walk on, keeping the fence close on your right, for 1.7 km.

Cross the road and walk through the gate opposite. Take the BRIDLEWAY MOLES CHAMBER ahead. At the next path junction keep left, MOLES CHAMBER. Follow a SSE course to the far corner of the field. Walk ahead in the same direction on BRIDLEWAY. Carry on via two blue waymarked gates to a memorial stone near a lane:

William Longe Oxenham
Esquire Lord of ye Manor
of High Bray 1742.

Turn sharply to your left and take the BRIDLEWAY through the wooden gate ahead. You now follow one of Britain's most ancient trackways, connecting the Midlands with Cornwall. The Saxons called it a harepath or military road. Follow it down to Mole's Chamber, boggy ground where a heap of grassy rubble marks the ruined Acland Arms, a 19th century inn.

Cross the brook. Keeping the brook on your left, follow the bridleway to the B3358. Turn left for the parking area.

Some other Bossiney books you may find useful

Walks books

Really short walks – Exmoor and Brendon
Exmoor pub walks
Shortish walks North Devon
North Devon pub walks
Really short walks North Devon
Shortish walks in North Devon
Shortish walks – Quantocks and Mendips

Guidebooks

Exmoor – a shortish guide
Lynton & Lynmouth – a shortish guide
Devon Beach and Cove Guide
The Somerset Coast – Beaches and Walks
Where to watch wildlife in Devon